# MEDIA LITERACY: THINKING ABOUT

**by**
**Annelle Houk**
**Carlotta Bogart**

Pflaum/Standard

Design and illustration by Tim Potter
Library of Congress Catalog Card Number 74-77021
ISBN 0-8278-0264-1
2   3   4   5   6   7   8   9

# Table of Contents

# Introduction

# 1

## "Thinking About"
## (Humans & Enimals)

by
H*Y*M*A*N  K*A*P*L*A*N

### 1.

Somtime I feel sad about how som people are living. Only sleeping eating working in shop. Not *thinking*. They are just like Enimals the same, which dont thinking also. Humans should not be like Enimals! They should *Thinking!* This is with me a deep idea.

Now we are having in school the axemination — a Comp. Mostly, will the students write a *story* for Comp. But I am asking, Why must allways be a story? Mr. P. must be sick and tierd from storys. Kaplan, be a man! No story! Tell better about *Thinking* something! Fine. Now I am thinking.

### 2.

In the recass was som students asking if is right to say Its Me or Its I — (because maybe we will have that question in axemination). Its Me or Its I — a planty hard question, no? Yes.

But it isnt so hard if we are *thinking about*! I figgure in this way:

If somebody is in hall besides my door, and makes knok, knok, knok; so I holler netcheral

"Whose there"? Comes the anser "Its Me." A fine anser!! Who is that Me anyho? Can I tell? No! So is Its Me no good.

Again is knok, knok, knok. And again I holler "Whose there"? Now comes the anser "Its I." So who is now that I?? Still can I (Kaplan) tell?? Ha! Umpossible!

*So it looks like is no anser.* (Turn around paige)

But must be *som kind anser*. So how we can find him out??? BY THINKING ABOUT. (Now I show how Humans isnt Enimals)

### 3.

If *I* am in hall and make knok, knok, knok; and I hear insite (insite the room) somebody hollers "Whose there"? — I anser strong *"Its Kaplan!"!!*

Now is fine! Plain, clear like gold, no chance mixing up Me, I, Ect.

By *Thinking* is Humans making big edvences on Enimals. This we call Progriss.

### T-H-E  E-N-D

ps. I dont care if I dont pass, I *love* this class.

From THE EDUCATION OF HYMAN KAPLAN by Leonard Q. Ross, copyright, 1937, by Harcourt Brace Jovanovich, Inc.; copyright, 1965, by Leo Rosten. Reprinted by permission of the publisher.

For Hyman Kaplan there was no received wisdom. No matter who told him what, every idea, any rule, any content had to be tested against his own experience and with his own reason. His essay entitled "Thinking About" is an excellent fictional piece of evidence that there is indeed a difference between being educated and being schooled.

Schooling produces horses with perfect gaits, children with accurate enunciation and grammar, and no square pegs. Education — literacy — produces nothing. Instead, it is the power that persons who develop it can exercise over their world and themselves. So defined, literacy becomes the individual's assertion of his power over his behavior — his refusal to permit his behavior to be modified without his conscious acquiescence. Literacy is independent behavior consciously shaping and being shaped by media of all kinds.

AH and CB

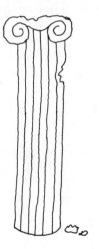

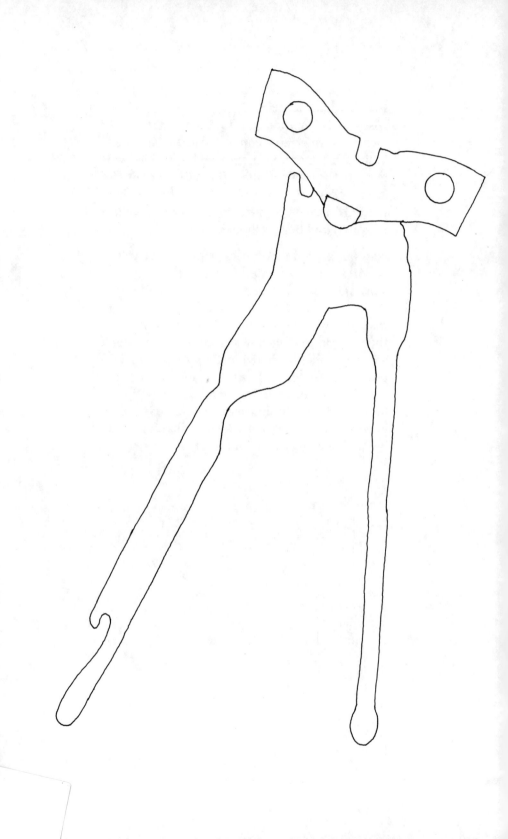

## Chapter 1: You Can If You Want To

So you're going to teach media. You have one camera but no film, the TV set is in the other pod, and this year's budget cuts eliminated paperbacks. But you have at least four walls, and if you want to begin media study there, you can start by listening to what the walls have to say.

Ask your students what one wall could say to another wall besides "Meet you at the corner." And then question what very different responses a single wall sends. Note the difference between what the wall's builder intended (probably "Keep on your side!") and the wall's own multiple messages of "Go around, over, under; walk on top, etc."

Continue to encourage your students to think aloud about what messages are sent by every other structure, every texture, every color, every sound in your particular classroom. For example, what is the seat in the classroom saying to the sitter? Be prepared for as many different answers as there are students because every receiver has a unique personal relationship to every medium.

What is the shoe saying to the foot? Or for that matter, is there evidence that the foot has communicated something to the shoe? And what has the shoe said to the floor? And has the floor answered?

Be prepared for chaos the first day you permit thinking about the learning environment instead of about recognizable subject matter.

Be prepared for some students' fury at being asked to think such stupid things when they could be learning something.

If to cut down on the noise level you shift from talking to writing, and if you want the flow of ideas to continue, be prepared not to grade the grammar or insult the sentence structure, and to tolerate the noise that will continue from the intense necessity of sharing discoveries too good to wait for permission. What will disappear temporarily will be discipline of the body (shut the mouth, keep the seat) and conformity of communication (put the period, spell the word) at the cost of the growing discipline of thought (open the ears, open the eyes, open the mind, move the muscle, feel the emotion).

Students will probably rate media class the

least useful, most interesting class — the one in which they learn the most personally that they need the least in school. Because it's fun, it can't be work. Because it's not work, it can't be useful; and besides, what kind of job would pay you to think like this anyway?

Make no mistake, however. Media study is a serious and sober subject. Therefore, homework must be assigned.

Everyone knows the importance of the printing press, but the can has been neglected. Therefore, ask every student to enlist the cooperation of his family in obtaining and eating the contents of a can of something. So that his family, too, can understand the seriousness of the assignment, require at least the following record to be kept for comparison and compilation by the whole class and later shared at home:

Who got the can?
Where?
At what cost?
Why that brand?
Why that size?
Who else touched the can between the shelf and the home if it was not home canned?
Who touched it at home, for what purposes, with what, and how?
What were the contents?
Geographically, where did the contents come from?
What happened to the empty can?

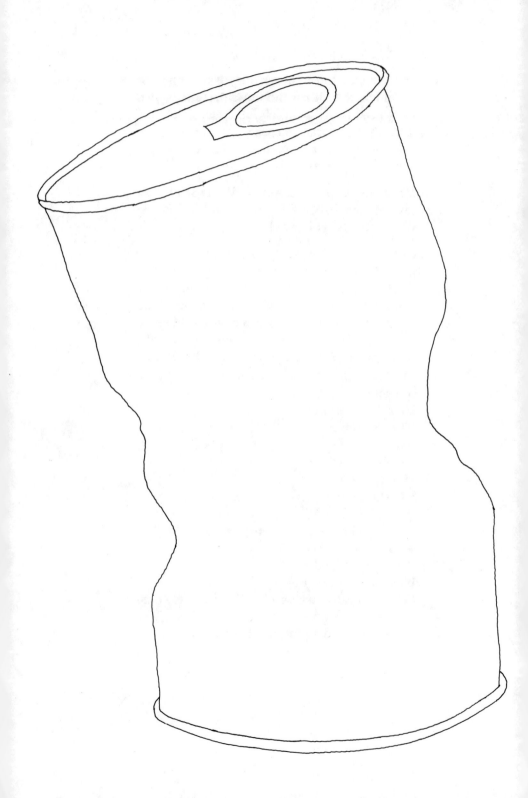

For economy, the same can can be used for further study if the student will bring both the can (cleaned) and its label to school; for cans are not merely containers of food for individuals. They affect the economy and the ecology. Where do they come from? Where do they go? How have cans affected our lives coming and going? Class projects to which all contribute can use those single cans to begin a whole semester's work in economics, art, human relations, psychology, consumer protection, international food production and marketing and distribution, etc.

Thinking about anything — even a can — will make us aware that that thing is a medium of communication. But any thing — even a can — will communicate itself as well as (or even instead of) that often simple message its inventor or first user intended. Furthermore, our use of anything — even a can — confers responsibility for all the messages of the medium — those intended and recognized and those hidden unsuspected in the nature of the medium.

## The Can as a Medium

In its structure the can carries messages about its physical nature — its demands of space, its strengths, its weaknesses. In its materials it carries messages of its derivation and its destiny. Its contents carry messages about

their production and processing. Its label
bears information and influences us to buy.

We consciously acknowledge some of the
can's messages when we choose to use it, but
by that use we also become responsible for all
the messages that the can carries — even those
of which we are not at all aware. Furthermore, again both consciously and uncon-
sciously, our use of cans comments on what
we value — time, convenience, etc. And the
messages that we impose on media or to
which we respond are often the least important that they carry.

### Note on Media Study Activities

Media study of its own nature can operate in
any medium or in many media and on many
levels simultaneously. The more consciously
one thinks about a medium, the more diversi-
fied his activity and his insight will become.
Whether an entire class, small groups, or
individuals carry out particular projects or
explore particular questions depends on the
unique conditions of time, space, materials,
and ability that exist in any particular school
situation.

What follows are suggestions that may lead to
traditional library research and business-letter
writing, to posters and other pop art, to film
making, to informational display and creative
commentaries — even to political action.

Ideally, media study is a success curriculum that permits a student to capitalize on his strongest ability while learning to shore up his weaknesses. Sometimes this means that the psychomotor student with little verbal ability teams with a very verbal student in constructing a three-dimensional word-picture-product project. A nonreader may be encouraged to use a tape recorder. A visually acute, shyly inarticulate student may produce a film which he augments only with music. A prime intention is that all participate and that all activities finally be shared successfully.

## THE BASIC CAN CURRICULUM

### CANalysis

1. What is a can? (Find the name and address of a major can manufacturer and write a letter of inquiry about film or print material that may be obtained that describes manufacturing processes and the variety of their products.)

2. What kinds of cans are there? (Collect cans of all shapes and sizes and construct a sculpture.)

3. What can be canned? (Make a collage of pictures from magazines of canned laughter, canned heat, canned salmon, etc.)

4. How do cans open? (Set up a display.)

5. Prepare a display of labels for the same product (peas?) produced and sold by differ-

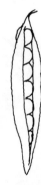

ent companies. Then analyze the market and the appeal of each product as determined by the label.

6. Survey a grocery store for the countries from which it stocks food and map them, preferably with pictures hand drawn or cut from magazines.

*CANformation*

1. Write a history of a/the can.

2. Make a slide show or film illustrating the importance of the can to your local community. (Gas being carried to stalled car, garbage can, oil drum, etc.)

3. Report on laws related to cans in your community. (Garbage disposal regulations, anti-littering laws, recycling requirements.)

4. Investigate the Oregon bottle law.

5. Is everything called canned, in a can? ("They canned my dad today." "Buy me a can of biscuits.")

## CANalogy

The can is one among many containers. How is it like and different from bottles, boxes, cars, computers, etc.? (Posters, collages, displays, slides and film, black-and-white single shots, abstractions, overhead projector overlays, opaque projector series, etc.)

## UnCANny Activities

1. Design pop-top-can ring jewelry or decorations.

2. Debate: Resolved, that the can is a major factor in the liberation of women.

3. Tape an interview with your garbage man about his entire day, particularly what he learns of people from their garbage.

4. Write a model ordinance for your local government requiring the distribution of drinks in returnable or recyclable containers.

5. Identify and interview major opponents to drink-container regulation.

6. Design a label intended to sell a new product of your choice.

7. For a can label that you imagine, write clear instructions for the use of the contents in a special recipe.

8. Invent a name for a canned food or some other product.

9. Study can pollution in your community (film, slides, black and white photos; tape-recorded commentary on a ride down the main street or by the nearest river).

10. Get down in the dumps.

You also can . . . .

## Chapter 2: Spit and Polish

Spit and polish is a term coined by soldiers who discovered that they got a higher shine on shoes and buckles for military inspections if they added a little spit to their polish.

A realistic teacher knows that many people — often even the administrators who ask for media curricula — are ambivalent about the value of a media curriculum. Therefore, knowing how to show off students' media work without either exploiting the students or prostituting the course is vital to the survival of the course and often to the success of the teacher in the eyes of outsiders. Deliberately planning to gain praise and to avoid criticism for media work requires an honest admission that the average adult and many students have to be sold that media units aren't a new kind of basket-weaving substitute for grammar or physics. And truth- fully, teachers' intelligence, discipline, integ- rity, and sweat are the only real protections against media students' substituting razzle-dazzle for substantial learning.

Fortunately, the nature of media tends to make the study of any medium yield a product — visible evidence of the nature of the student's involvement with the medium. At the end of a study of 'film, for example, there usually is at least a single photograph if not a sequence or an entire film that is student-made. Everyone is visually experienced to some degree if not visually literate. Therefore, that visible student product represents to students, teachers, parents, and administrators a measurable investment of time and energy and at least to some extent an understanding of process or content that can be evaluated.

The job of the teacher is to be sure that potential critics (evaluators) of student media projects appreciate the learning that the product has permitted rather than judge the perfection of the products.

In other words, an effective media teacher polishes the context of the learning.

Where the talent of the students is such that the product itself shines, the teacher's job may well be to keep the observer's perspective clear that the edge one product has over the quality of another is usually a matter of a student's native ability — not just the learning. What needs appreciation may be the projects of students who have learned more than their skills can exhibit. In other words, the product sometimes isn't much but the learning always is.

Where learning is valued most — more than perfection of product — a group effort that fails of its intent may be as successful as the product that special talent makes superior as a product.

For example, suppose a group decides to make a film with music and voice-over narration. Suppose further that filmmaking, recording, and writing and reading narration all are new ventures for everyone. The product may end up a combination of sounds and sights that no one but the students themselves appreciate or value. What the media teacher needs to do is to help the students and others evaluate what the students have learned from their successes and their errors, not merely to take a look at and/or listen to the product and judge it.

If the group has learned only to take the risk of learning — of experimenting — of creating — any project is a success. In fact, to encourage exploration the teacher must be careful not to reward students for replication of processes in which they already excel. However, neither must a student be required never to contribute what he already does best just because he needs to extend his learning.

Successful products tend to result from carefully planned group work.

Successful learning as well as display often results from combining persons who complement one another, learn from the facilities of each other, and end up with a better performance than any can manage alone in a new exploration. That means that a person who writes well may write for a group that contains nonwriters who are good artists, narrators or photographers. They, in turn, contribute what the writer lacks in experience or skill.

The students themselves make the best possible presenters of their work.

An outsider, exposed to the enthusiastic presentation of projects by their makers, will recognize the difference between conventional success and media learning. When students explain without either apology or excessive pride how they have tried to accomplish something important to them, the observer can realize the necessity of an atmosphere that rewards the willingness to explore and discourages the dully safe exercise.

Media classes may be the first classes in which adults have an opportunity to observe what happens to students freed to make errors by contracting to work as best they can with no threat of failure if their learning succeeds but their product fails. What may seem most remarkable is that in such a nonthreatening atmosphere there are so many surprising successes.

The very evidence that a student is carrying out his work as he promised to do is itself a powerful selling tool with parents and administrators. If each student can be helped to learn to log his own or his group's planning, procedures, and production, the log itself can become a tool for thinking regardless of whether the students work toward a poem, a poster, a lighting technique, a can collection, or a display. Ideally, however, a log is not a record for show-and-tell but is a means for identifying what goes well and what may be improved.

A media class may also be the first learning situation where some adults see judgment of student work strictly restricted to assessment in relation to a learning objective selected by the student. What he is to present publicly should always be assigned in a medium in which he feels confident even while he risks himself. A medium in which he knows he fails to perform adequately should never be the major medium that he presents publicly or on which his work is judged.

Suppose, for example, that a student plans his study to end with a tin-can sculpture. Since his learning is to be evaluated — not his log — he can get exercise in writing without fearing that his inability to write will be confused with failure of his thought or work.

Another need for media work is time for groups to plan and carry out their projects. Students sometimes need more than scheduled class time for this. Usually there is no more school time available. Partly there is no time because every experienced teacher has had to learn to guard his own class time from intrusions from other subjects if he is to accomplish his own course objectives.

An activity that will generate acceptance of media is to have the students involve their other teachers in the activities that link media objectives and those of more conventional disciplines.

The most important in-school selling point for media is students' involvement of their teachers in interdisciplinary activities where the teachers can see math applied in English and writing done well in physics and history graphed or dramatized. There is no sounder proof of successful teaching than to see objectives of one field fulfilled in another.

Going interdisciplinary is just one outreach of media. Ideally, good media projects involve the home and the community without draining either. Imagine a parent's actually being asked his opinion even if the purpose is to let a son or daughter practice taping an interview. Most doctors, lawyers, merchants, chiefs will give time to young people who really care what such professional persons think or do in their work or their civic activities. Giving business and industry and services and organized religion a first-hand look at serious students having fun learning about the real world is an excellent way to establish good community rapport with schools.

## Media Relationships

Mass media — print, film, TV, radio — have a bad name as manipulators. What better way can the schools inform the public that students are learning to use rather than be used by media than to involve the public in the students' work?

Furthermore, once media are thought of more broadly as all substances, principles, and structures that can be arranged or operated to communicate, media integrate rather than isolate both different disciplines and individuals.

## HELP OFFERED

### Tape

— how to do any media project for a media library other students can use.

— steps for teaching science experiments to other students.

— interviews with school visitors, career experts, celebrities in town, etc.

— panel discussions and group interviews (simulated TV news conferences, game shows).

— a no-word sound track for a short story.

*Talk*

— to younger students informally or formally about what the next division of their education will be like.

— to share special skills with others (tutor in your best subject, teach a craft during an activity period or at a community center, explain to a group of senior citizens something unusual like taxidermy that you have had experience in).

*Film*

— school sports for team analysis and local TV.

— pictures of people, events, and sports at school for the yearbook, school and local newspapers.

— a silent movie, a parody of a soap opera, a song, an idea, an emotion, how to do anything.

## Talent

— Form a media talent pool. (Make available to teachers, students, administrators a card index of schedules and phone numbers of student poster artists, photographers, projector operators, etc.).

— Make a public relations team available to all school departments to help devise publicity for events in the school and community.

## Design

— program covers and posters for school activities.

— a computer program for composing poetry, solving paperwork bottlenecks concerning registration, etc.

— polls to survey students, parents and other community members on current issues.

## HELP WANTED

— from the art department to demonstrate silk screen printing for two-color posters.

— from business and industry to explain career options and requirements.

— from people in the community to share special skills with classes.

— from businesses who will offer on-the-job training to students who want or need to work while they go to school.

## GETTING IT ALL TOGETHER

### Plan

— a media festival in the spring to exhibit outstanding work from all areas of the school (carpentry, welding, art, sewing, dance, music, speech, film, etc.)

### Display

— all the media and tools peculiar to each section of each department in the school (thread, scissors, patterns, yard goods in clothing; paint, brushes, posterboards, glues in art; mops, cleaners, vacuums in maintenance; etc.).

### Share

— your private laughter over your biggest failure in media projects; the funniest misspelling, typing or printing; your best wrong answers to questions never asked . . . .

## OPEN INVITATION

*Post*

— on doors times and kinds of media displays to which visitors are welcome.

*Write*

— formal and informal invitations to fit the medium and the occasion.

— a 30-second intercom announcement for an event (media's or anyone's).

— forgotten staff (nurses, secretaries, custodians) when you send media invitations.

— community individuals and mass media to share time, fun and skills with students.

## Chapter 3: Sermons in Stones

When we do something acceptably normal like studying rocks in geology, we look at rocks in terms of principles that someone else has derived and that we are taught. We feel quite comfortable thinking about the records of time in rock formations and even carbon dating of fossils we may be lucky enough to find. But suppose Shakespeare was right and there are sermons in stones. What if any old rock can preach?

The idea of stones' containing sermons suggests that all nature — and all that man has made from the materials of the earth — can communicate. If so, how can people learn to hear silent sermons?

Perhaps we go walking barefoot and step on a rock. Without question, our feet get a number of messages, relay them to our brains, and our minds make patterns out of those messages. But the rock has not merely spoken of itself.

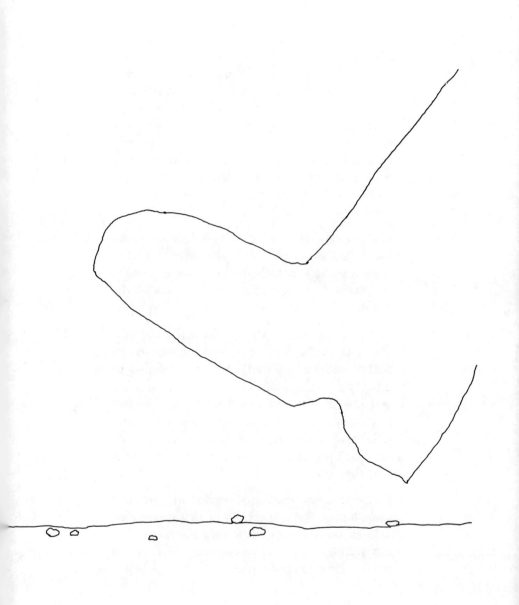

It also has caused our feet to speak of their nature. The messages received and translated into meaning, we then respond to the rock and to our feet. We move the rock, walk around it, put shoes on and ignore it, press the rock down until it is level with the rest of the ground, or put many other rocks beside that one and perhaps seal them all together with cement. So we must have read sermons in stones and in feet; and in turn we have spoken to the stones of what we have learned about both them and our relationship to them.

Presumably, we are as knowledgeable about rocks as we are about any other natural phenomenon on earth — and we are beginning to extend our knowledge to the rocks of the moon.

We have discovered that rocks make durable, efficient walls and that some rocks make better walls than others. We have learned to grind up rocks themselves and bind natural and imitation rocks together in what we call permanent structures. But walls still crack and fall. And then they act like rocks in total disregard of man's announcement to them that they are walls.

We have discovered that rocks will burn — some better than others. Some day we may be able to convert any rock into its energy for our purposes. We transport some of the coal to the furnace and produce heat and hence energy. We transport some of the coal to the alveoli of the lungs and produce disease and death.

The rock acts according to its nature in a wall, in a lung, in a furnace. Only when it is broken down in its composition — as by burning or chemical action — does its nature change. And then we must deal with the nature of the natural thing to which we have converted it.

It is the nature of water to run down a hill. It is the nature of a hill to transport down the water that it cannot absorb. Man cuts down trees and builds concrete and asphalt ribbons and buildings where trees stood. And the rain falls, and the water runs down man's impervious hills into nature's streams or man's lakes and they overflow. Sometimes the water washes away man's roads and buildings.

We want a farm, so we find the richest land. We plant crops on that delta in disregard of the natural processes of erosion that produced it in the first place. And the rains descend and the floods come and the farm is washed away. We find a beautiful rocky canyon and build our house high on an escarpment of it. And the earth rumbles and our house falls. And these we call natural disasters.

Man takes natural substances, transforms them into fuels, and burns them in cars that run up and down those non-absorbing hills. The cars emit wastes because they do not

consume the fuels entirely. The wastes that
are heavier than air fall to the ground, run
down with the rain, and concentrate to
poison fish, men, and other animals whose
bodies are not designed to handle the nature
of those displaced natural substances. Parti-
cles and gases lighter than air rise, disperse,
and linger so that we and trees and animals
may breathe them. And we call this pollution.

## The Morality of Stones

Shakespeare implies that there is some kind of
moral lesson in stones — a notion of what is a
right and what is a wrong relationship of man
and stones. In other words, if we people are
to get along with stones, we have to know
what we are doing when we adapt them to us.
The basic sermon in a stone seems to be that
we establish a right relationship with stones or
accept the consequences of our ignorance or
our willful violation of the nature of stones.

Perhaps Shakespeare meant in part that in
nature we can read man himself. Since man's
mind grows from the patterns derived from
his experience both of the real and the
imaginary world — the world of sensory
experience and of concepts he formulates
from experience — the logic of man derives
from nature. Furthermore, what a man makes
or an idea that he conceives also has a nature
and a reality of its own once it comes into
existence.

Man thinking is in a very real sense man learning to read stones well enough that he can both adapt stones to his purposes and adapt himself to the nature of stones.

## THE NATURAL CURRICULUM

### Easy-To-Read Sermons

1. What rocks are valuable? (Arrange rock samples or descriptions according to various values — usefulness, beauty, etc.).

2. What is the relation of roads to rocks? (Compare geographical, topographic, and road maps.)

3. What rocks contribute to your local economy? (See the Yellow Pages; make some calls; visit quarries, jewelers, etc.)

4. Read a slice of petrified wood, a geode, obsidian, sandstone.

5. What does the San Andreas Fault say?

6. Study precipitation in your area over the past fifty years. (See weather department records. Ask a lunberyard for a cross section of a fifty-year-old tree. Interview local senior citizens about their memories of floods and erosion from personal observation. Interrelate the information.)

7. Does a glacier know when it is about to become an iceberg?

8. How does a sea shell roar?

*Preach to the People*

1. as a blade of grass (how you grow, how you nourish horses, how you expire).

2. as a seed (popcorn, peanut, poppy, pine).

3. as a drop of rain (hailstone, snowflake, etc.).

4. as a cloud (cumulus, nimbus, etc.).

5. as a virus, a crystal, a bacterium.

*Famous Misreadings*

1. The *Titanic* is an unsinkable ship.

2. The world is flat.

3. The sun sets.

4. Manned flight will never exceed the speed of sound.

5. No one will ever hit more home runs than Babe Ruth.

6. No person will ever run the one-minute mile.

*Nature-ally*

1. food
2. clothing
3. shelter
4. reproduction
5. the windmill
6. solar energy

### The Nature of Change

1. peneplain (Forecast the levelling of the Rocky Mountains, the Himalayas, etc.)

2. the Grand Canyon (Photograph your own sand pile. Collect photos or maps of any one place over a period of time.)

3. mountain building (volcanos, continental drift, faults, plate tectonics, glaciers)

4. birth, life, and death (of anything, anyone. From your family photograph album illustrate the cycle with a relative.)

5. How do you know the Mississippi is "*old* man river"?

6. Explore the geological history of your own area.

7. Use time-lapse photography (crystal growth, flowers blooming, a fire, a sunrise).

### The Changes of Nature

1. the bulldozer

2. the dam

3. the builder (Study the effect of city weight on earthquake probability, the water table, weather.)

4. the hybridizer (beardless wheat, corn blight)

5 the cloud seeder

6. the fertilizer

7. the explosive

8. the geneticist (beefalo, mules, etc.)

9. the atom smasher

*Natural Metonymy*

1. satellite photographs (geological structures, mineral deposits, vegetation, crop conditions)

2. amplification (Listen to an insect, the grass, a cat's purr, a heartbeat. Explore experiments in sound-proof environments.)

3. chemical analysis (Read the priorities of man in the chemistry of your nearest stream or lake.)

4. holography (Compare and contrast a photograph and a hologram.)

5. reconstruction (a drop of water to an ocean, a grain of sand into a mountain, a cell into a body, a bone into a skeleton)

6. parallel records (a rain storm — barometric pressures, wind velocities, cloud formations, responses of insects, plants, soil; Abe Lincoln — his letters, fictional and factual biography, photographs, a play, poetry, etc.)

## Chapter 4: Two Senses Worth

The reason to study mass media at all is to understand both how mass media control us and how we may control them. All mass media depend on the two senses of hearing and sight. Yet, if we had only hearing and sight, we would reduce our awareness of the world almost completely to intellectual observation and/or emotional reaction. Among what we would lose would be texture, depth, and our own motions and actions that test and unify our major knowledge of the physical world. Limited to detecting sights and sounds, we would become observers of life rather than participants in it.

Mass media seem to threaten to make us passive. However, because mass media make our minds so active, almost no medium can keep a person passive more than temporarily. Furthermore, print, radio, recordings, film, and television have in common an ability to expand our experience in a shorter time and across greater physical space than our own actions permit.

The greater the number and variety of experiences, direct or vicarious, the greater our growth of mind. The greater the frequency of media and vicarious experience, the more deeply we expand our understanding.

Few of us will fly around the world, set foot on the moon, operate the world's largest telescope, discover a natural medication of the value of penicillin, or write a modern *Paradise Lost.* Yet one or more of the mass media can sooner or later permit us to participate at least vicariously in both the discoveries and the creations that we can comprehend through sight or sound. Most importantly, that acceleration of participation in the experience of others increases the quantity and quality of our own experience. And the rapidity of our personal growth is in direct proportion precisely to the quantity and quality of our experience.

Just as the person who invented the can revolutionized the eating habits of the industrialized world, so the inventors of alphabets, the printing press, the telegraph, radio, tape, and television revolutionized the intellectual consumption of everyone exposed to them. And the inventors of eye-ear media neither foresaw nor can control the contents of print, radio, and TV any more than can the can's inventor control the contents of the world's cans today.

With sufficient money and opportunity a consumer now can taste chocolate covered ants, beer, bacon rinds, vegetable soup, and any other nourishing or idiosyncratic or debauching product produced in the world that his curiosity, his cultivated craving, or his normal appetite desires. Mass media make it equally possible to feed or glut the mind with sensation or repetition and to indulge one's mental appetites.

The analogy between the consumption of food and the consumption of media suggests further similar behaviors. Pantry critics may sneer at shelves stocked with commonplace canned goods and regret the lack of taste of mass buyers in relation to the critics' own views of what foods are valuable. Media critics, censors, and media merchants tend to make similar judgments of the tastes of consumers of mass media. Ironically, those persons who sneer most at mass taste seem often to work hardest to manipulate the masses and subsequently to make the most profit from that manipulation. For example, the advertiser who sneers at the media consumer often does the most to create the bad taste he sneers at. Sometimes he even refuses to support the consumer when he shows excellent taste.

Studying mass media requires the ability to sample and assess the content of mass media without condescension or automatic approval. In other words, exploration of the mass media ideally should be as open to discovery as is sensory exploration of the physical world. Such exploration with freedom is extremely difficult to manage, however, because of the conscious and unconscious power needs culturally built into each generation of media consumers. Those needs tend to cause persons to defend or attack various media on the basis of which media or medium each has been taught to accept or respect.

Probably the first person to devise a symbol to substitute for spoken words sold his medium to someone else on the condition that the buyer agree that the symbols meant what the originator said they did. Presumably the originator sought to market his symbol system partly to improve his own communication with them by standardizing the medium and hence making it easier to transport information accurately over longer times and distances.

Once accepted, the symbol system has to be taught formally — as the spoken word did not — because the symbol system was arbitrarily imposed, not mutually generated. Therefore education began as a means for transmitting the agreed symbol system to people born later into the society that had accepted it. The

standardization of words necessary to control-
ling the symbol system and education's control of the people using it conflicted with the
natural fluidity of spoken words in daily
usage. For example "It" used to be considered as illiterate as "ain't" until the stand-
ardizers accepted "it" by force of spoken
frequency. To permit the symbol system to
be asserted as superior to the spoken language, the symbol makers constantly had to
keep standardizing more and more words
and incorporating them into the system so
that the diversity of the symbol system could
compete successfully with that of the spoken
language. For another instance, today's writ-
ten language has to keep up with space
technology; so we all know how to spell
NASA and read about sky-labs.

What was lost when the symbol system
standardized meaning was each individual's
unique view of his own experience. If the
individual accepted the symbol system, he
agreed to adapt himself and work within the
system. If he could not adequately express
himself in that medium, he could try to adapt
the system by devising new symbols (usually
by raiding the spoken vocabulary) or changing
old ones. If he could neither successfully
adapt himself nor change the system, his
alternatives were to reject his education for
the imprecision but the freedom of the
spoken language or to invent another medium
to add to the standardized one.

Persons deriving their social power from their command of a medium have always fought change even when the unchanged medium could not meet new needs adequately. Therefore, their very efforts to maintain the status quo have hastened if not provoked the development of new media. Furthermore, persons dependent for power on the preservation of their medium have almost universally fought to maintain exclusive control of communication. To exist at all, each new medium has in turn had to fight the old as if to replace it totally. Instead, each medium, new or old, has maintained at least a part of its functions and supplements or complements other media.

The spoken word was not replaced by print. Print was not replaced by radio. Television has not killed off either film or radio or print. However, each new medium has caused the revision of the roles of other media. No man can any more be truly literate if he depends solely on any single medium for his information. Neither can any man or group of people control a medium. Sooner or later, by access, numbers, and individuality, the masses regain control of every medium. Then media become creative extensions of individuals who can limit the power of the media over them and use the media for their purposes.

*Print*

Print is the most individualized mass medium because any interested person can seek and find some sort of print material suited to his age, ability, and interest. Its defect is that full comprehension of print requires the reader to bring as much experience and attention to reading as the writer brought to composition. Because reading print alone is a most complex symbolic process carried on completely intellectually, it requires the development of precise skills primarily through incremental repetition. The rate of that development apparently is so unique to each person that no one knows yet how to supply reading experience in appropriate individualized quantities of the right level at the right rate and time to permit mass print literacy.

Because print is a linear medium, it has a beginning and an end both in time and space; and its line determines the sequence, hence the time of the contact with content. Syntax or formulae manipulate that order to put ideas in positions early or late where their content or function is either stressed or deemphasized. A writer through grammar controls the unique structures that play down or build up the relative structure of ideas.

Because of its flexibility, print has an almost infinite capacity to store disciplined information, ideas, and invention. Its effect is to freeze concepts and effects in immutable but varied forms. An accomplished reader has time to read and reread and compare until the cold content of words and other symbols comes alive in his own active mind. Therefore, print is the major mass medium yet developed for disciplined logical and creative thought.

Ultimately, the most comprehensive and the most complicated ideas are extremely short in print. $E=MC^2$ is perhaps the supreme example of the severe simplicity of fully clarified thought made permanent in print. Those five symbols condense whole fields of knowledge and make possible explanation of a host of hypotheses scarcely dreamed of before Einstein's simple statement of their relationship.

The strictly utilitarian mass uses of print are identification, information, and selling. They require the minimum ability to read. Often they are only fragments that get their context not from sentence structure but from location. Identification signs, for example, are nouns or noun clusters on streets or buildings they name or that point to services or products visibly available nearby. Often the sign is merely an attention device to draw the eye to the physical context. A reader would recognize a fence company once a sign drew his eye to the stock of fencing.

Other signs that primarily give directions use an action verb with the reader the understood subject. Increasingly these signs are being replaced by international nonverbal symbols. Print information signs also are being replaced by these universally recognized picture symbols (for example, school crossing, rest room).

Advertising signs use a minimum of print — often fragments such as incomplete comparisons and nonreferring pronouns that cause the reader to supply personally his association with the picture. That association usually gives the print what context it does have. Reading advertising print always means reading the total context in which the print appears.

The rate at which a reader acquires information through print depends on the intelligence, age, and variety of experiences of each individual. The prime factors seem to be easy and constant access to and experience with books, magazines, and newspapers. The best readers now grow up immersed also in media other than print.

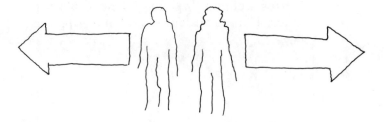

*GO TO PRESS*

1. Put English in the order of other languages (posters)

2. Experiment with reverse English (mirror write, right to left; make a concrete poem; tennis)

3. The power of invisible print
   1. property lines
   2. maps
   3. reading between the lines (semantics)
   4. caste, class, monetary systems
   5. flight patterns
   6. international date line
   7. equator
   8. human rights

4. Color the news (With overlays, crayon, paint, distinguish what news is local, national, foreign and international)
   (Color who, what, when, where, how and why in the first paragraph of an/each article.)

5. What do you read? (Make your own paper including only what you read normally from a daily paper.)

6. A cross section of opinion (Make a collage of editorials and cartoons representing opposing views).

*Display Advertising*

(Pull from the paper all of the ads on a particular product.)

1. Who is selling what? (Analyze the dealers — photograph their headquarters and compare the size of the companies with the size of the ads.)

2. Who is buying? (Identify the market.)

3. What's the pitch? (safety, economy, luxury, gifts, fear, sex)

4. What's the date got to do with the pitch? (Mother's Day, Fourth of July, Father's Day, Washington's birthday)

5. What's the pitch got to do with the news? (new auto emission standards, the economy)

6. So what else is on the page? (Do the surrounding articles and ads sell it or fight it?)

*Classified*

1. How are people and things segregated in your paper?

2. What other than words identifies the classifications? Who needs them?

3. "Lost and Found" (Who lost what, valued why, and how much? Write a short story.)

4. "Educational Opportunities" — who's selling what? (Film a fantasy of the student who believes the ad.)

5. "Help Wanted" (Chart the pay for the first five jobs under each help wanted classification)

(Write a job description of one typical job from each classification)

(Rank the first five jobs from each classification from most to least amount of education required)

(Stage three job interviews for any job: one over-qualified, one under-qualified, one qualified)

(Contact several agencies and chart their fees in relation to tthe income of the persons for whom they find jobs. For whom are fees most likely to be paid by the prospective employer?)

*Reading Context*

Who advertises in what?

1. Analyze the "Help Wanted" sections of three national circulation magazines.

2. What kinds of products advertise in any single magazine? Why? (Write the sales manager of the magazine for a market breakdown of subscribers).

### *Is What You See What You Get?*

1. For a whole series of ads for different products draw to scale the size of the product as presented in relation to the size of the ad.

2. Collect a series of predominantly picture ads using the same appeal. (sex, fresh air, etc. Code them and remove all evidence of the product in print or picture. Prepare a matching product identification test for the class and chart the accuracy of their scores.)

3. List the products in your medicine cabinet that are nationally advertised.

### *Sound*

A nonreader can listen with understanding to oral materials of any sophistication for which he develops a listening vocabulary. The difficult translation steps reading requires are eliminated when words spoken or read or sung are transmitted by radio or recorded on records or tape. Therefore, the listener often can understand concepts he may not have the facility to express for himself either in speech or writing. Furthermore, spoken or sung words supply interpretation and emphasis that print requires a reader to determine for himself with the aid of his mental experience alone. The speaker's oral abilities may restrict the listener's consideration of alternate potential meaning of words much more than even

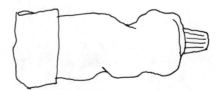

emotionally colored words can in print. In fact, a listener may be led to his understanding of words by the emotional power of the voice rather than by the content of the words.

The effect of the total context of sound on the listener's understanding perhaps is most clear in popular music. Often the meaning of words sung matters very little. They may not even be understood until they have been repeated many times, most likely in a rather short period of time. Nevertheless, the meaning of words under these circumstances seems to have unconscious influence similar to the effect of visual images repeated in film too few frames to be seen consciously. Also, pitch, stress and volume of sound evoke emotion much in the way touch does. Of all the senses, hearing and touch seem closest to the emotions and least filtered through reason. Perhaps that is why feelings and images in response to sound and touch are so highly personal, so difficult to share in any alternate media, and so privately valuable.

Undoubtedly media dependent on sound alone, plus the kinesthetic effect of vibration other than on the ear, do indeed have strong emotional appeal. This power derives primarily from the freedom of the listener to use his personal experience to supply every other aspect than sound required to make meaning from sound waves. That very direct, intensely

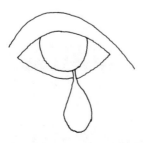

personal contribution of the listener to the medium is reflected in the high degree of selectivity the listener exercises over sources of sound and the sound content with which he fills his listening time. Witness both the variety of listening fare selectively offered by a great number of AM and FM radio stations in any large market and the unprecedented popularity of tapes and recordings across the entire spectrum of available sounds.

Tapes, recordings, concerts and other forms of exact repetition permit a listener to develop the same kind of aural sophistication that rereading print permits the reader's intellect. When that repetition is quadrasonic with the volume high, the sound cocoon of the listener isolates him almost totally in personal experience.

The rate at which information is acquired through sound media is much faster than through print. Nevertheless, until the sense experience itself is repeated often enough, it cannot rise to a level of consciousness that permits the listener the kind of conscious control he can exercise sooner over the content of print.

*SOUND ON*

1. Tape vocal expressions of emotions with words garbled. (anger, fear, love, excitement, etc.)

2. Listen to the audio on TV without the video and see how well you can identify the action. What does music add to dramas, commercials, soap operas?

3. Identify songs by rhythm tapped on a desk, lyrics of a little known verse, or listening when instrumental volume is louder than the vocal.

4. How fast can you identify groups by a phrase or two of their music? TV programs by their themes?

5. Change music into light.

6. How well can you identify common sounds recorded on tape?

7. What can a Moog synthesizer imitate?

8. Simulate a sports announcer, a disc jockey, an MC, a news announcer.

9. Tape an interview. Read the phone book like a disk jockey, news announcer, politician.

10. Write a paper after hearing the directions only once.

11. Tape yourself telling someone how to get to your home from school. (Follow your own directions.)

*Radio*

1. Does what you like matter?
   (What station(s) do you turn on regularly?)
   (What music do they sell to what audience?)
   (What products do they sell?)
   (Who owns the station?)
   (If you stopped listening, what would you lose? What would the station lose?)

2. What do you not support by not listening to other stations (music, sports, news, religions, organizations, companies)?

3. Write a job description for a disc jockey.

4. News    Survey and analyze the time spent by stations reporting news each day.
   (How much time goes for local, national, global reporting?)
   (How often is the same event repeated identically?)
   (How long does it take to get news of a local event? a national one?)
   (How much news comes from UPI, AP, NEA and local investigation?)
   (Who decides what is news?)
   (Who sponsors news with what products aimed at whom?)
   (How controversial is coverage of local issues?)
   (Can you tell the announcer's biases?)

*Film*

Film was the visual motion medium of the pre-electronic age. Television has not replaced it even though film and TV have adopted and adapted each other. And electronic developments have extended its field to include the micro and macro worlds.

Regardless of whether a film is intended as art, entertainment, or instruction, it unrolls from a reel in linear frames each of which is as stopped an action as a noun is. Motion in film is an illusion. The capacity of film to repeat without change the same sequence and content of visual experience makes it the pictorial counterpart of print. Film literature permits the development of what might by analogy be called a grammar, a syntax and a rhetoric. In that sense, the study of film becomes to some degree potentially scientific or at least systematic.

On a practical level film is the medium worth a thousand words a still frame. Set in motion, a few feet of film says much more than a few feet of print. Without question what is seen clearly in its details — particularly if it is seen repeatedly from the same and different points of view — becomes patterned mental information. Such visually established patterns can much more easily be translated into words than words can be translated into mental images. If direct or vicarious experience has been derived solely from words, imagining touch, hearing, smell or clear mental pictures is particularly difficult, if not impossible. A thousand words are never enough to reproduce a picture with the detail of film.

Both words and film, however, can serve to make the present permanent when it becomes the past.

Despite its potential power to inform, to persuade, to inspire – despite all its potential, film cannot take the place of words for two prime reasons.

First, no matter how carefully a filmmaker believes that he has focused on a subject or objects or action, he cannot control the focus of the individual viewer. Just as the point of view of the cameraman (the film editor, etc.) will screen out of his consciousness much of what the camera records, so each viewer's point of view may cause him to focus on something in the foreground or background that the filmmaker considers peripheral.

Second, the viewer will see what he knows how to see, and his experience may not be such that he is even capable of seeing what the filmmaker thinks he records and can himself see in his film.

Because individual point of view in both making and viewing film is so difficult to analyze, much less anticipate, the power of film probably is predominantly unconscious.

When words are added to film, they help to fix the viewer's attention on the filmmaker's intended emphasis. When music is added, it helps produce the emotion intended to enhance that focus. No matter how great the control of words or music, the viewer still will see what he will see. And his most permanent learning may be what he absorbs peripherally.

Film initially kept sizes in relatively realistic proportions. When films began to be made expressly for television, this distinction largely was lost. When a mountain and a molehill are shown as if of equal size, only viewer experience can compensate for the loss of realistic proportions. On the other hand, films made for television have helped viewers of the news handle the sight of the whole world on the small screen.

## ROLL ON

### Advertising

1. How do movie theaters promote their coming attractions? (See a movie and prepare the print teaser for the film.)

2. What name products are identifiable in the film? (automobiles, cigarettes, etc.)

3. What local and name products are advertised as in the lobby between films? What products are advertised in the lobby itself?

4. How much TV advertising is film?

5. Compare advertising costs on film and on TV tape.

6. Decide what camera to buy (on the basis of advertising available)
for your father.
for a ten-year-old.
for a portrait photographer.
for rich you.

*Developing Illusion*

1. How authentic is the science of human and animal behavior in Tarzan films?

2. Study the elements of plot in films.

3. Compare print and film versions of plays, novels, and short stories. (How is time sequence different, what does sound add besides the dialogue, and how do camera angles and lighting affect mood?)

4. Make a documentary of any literature, science, social studies, or news event.

5. Trace universal themes in film and in literature (isolation, identity, discovery, etc.).

6. Make an animated film.

7. Compare how different students arrange the sequence of action using the same set of photographs or pictures.

8. Decide what photographic action was recorded on film at a particular point and what
would happen if the action resumed.

9. Photograph one subject and develop one
satisfactory print.

10. Study student or professional prints to find
good uses of composition, framing, texture,
etc. for character, action, scene, etc.

11. How is film made? In what sizes? For what
purposes?

12. What should one know about film to take
pictures on the moon?

*Television*

Television cools to some extent the listener-
viewer's emotional involvement with the
medium. Primarily this cooling derives from
television's providing, as does film, visual
images that the imagination of both the
reader of print and the listener to sound
media must contribute from their own experiences. A member of the television audience
becomes to a great degree precisely that: an
anonymous observer belonging to an uniden-
tified audience. But his observation is with
two senses, not the single sense implied by the
inaccurate term "television viewer."

The viewer-listener may react with fascination
to what he sees and hears, but even an intense

reaction still reflects his distance from the televised experience. One of the unique effects of television comes from that felt distance. While radio listeners often have great difficulty distinguishing fact from fiction if they tune in in the middle of a program, experienced members of the TV audience usually can detect the difference as soon as the sound and the picture are both on. The quantity of their television experience has taught them what the average reader of print knows: the patterns of fact and the patterns of fiction.

The television audience member develops another and more sophisticated level of discrimination more rapidly than the reader or the listener develops it. Even with entertainment programming, he soon judges the reliability of the context. His emotional distance plus his at least unconscious discrimination of patterns of reliable fact transform television into a potent educator. Even the least creative, most stereotyped, most repetitious programs sooner or later expand the individual consciousness particularly by expanding vocabulary. The television listener's vocabulary grows far faster in number and variety than does that of a reader or a listener — each of whom is restricted to intake through a single sense. A visual context for words heard reduces the frequency of repetition necessary for them to become standardized. Where the listener-viewer knows the characters, the setting, and the attitudes he can expect, his attention is attracted primarily by the unexpected and his experience grows with each moderate change or startling event.

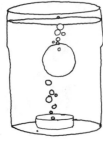

Since it is the nature of mind to make meaning of experience, perhaps TV commercial techniques inadvertently make the greatest single contribution to the growth of literacy. Repetition and concept integration are their special forte.

Television programming in general provides the average person a much greater quantity of much more accurate and varied content than any previous generation has had access to through any other single medium or combina-. tion of media.

Television can expand experience vicariously faster also than any other medium, not only with greater uniformity of viewer-listener learning but also without most of the enormously complex cognitive skills required by print. Furthermore, as the consciousness of a member of the TV audience grows, selectivity tends to emerge, much as it does in the taste of persons using and being used by print and sound media.

The new generation that has grown up with the television always on has developed selectivity with a speed that probably is vastly underestimated, primarily because the quantity of apparently indiscriminant viewing seems to contradict the possibility of selectivity. However, a medium-literate person swallows only what he chooses of all that quantity he submits to.

Stop-action replays and the repetition videotape makes possible will speed the development of an even more sophisticated television literacy. Much as being able to reread words makes a man more literate than if he can analyze what he merely hears, even repeatedly, so being able to videotape television fare will put the analysis of television under his control.

The more literate he becomes in each medium and the more media in which he becomes literate, paradoxically, the broader his tastes will be but the more selective he will naturally become.

For all the visual variety of television plus the juxtaposition of sights and sounds, television still is a medium linear in time and heavily dependent on both the spoken and the printed word. Most action still proceeds by line of sight in space sequences, and words predominantly follow the linear sequence of print or speech. The printed word itself is still essential for advertising on TV.

No doubt a major effect of television is emotional and is evoked by television's visual vividness. But with rare exceptions, words — and those words at least initially on paper —

control the design even of visual sequence. Except for live coverage of spontaneous events by more than one camera, the print of writers, directors, producers, sponsors, and governmental control agencies still controls television. And even that live coverage often reflects selections suggested and predicted in print.

## RESHAPING ACTION

### The Information Tube

1. Simulate motion by sequencing cartooned characters before a background scene to tell a story. (Recreate literature, make a commercial, simulate or animate an historical or scientific event.)

2. Compare the time it takes you to identify a TV program by its theme music with identification times required by (1) a major character's repeating phrases he habitually uses; (2) viewing pictures of major characters out of costume; (3) viewing pictures of the program's setting.

3. Interview a marketing expert at a TV station to find out how time is sold.

4. Analyze the cost of local advertising on the basis of your interview with the TV marketing expert (a product, a particular time, frequency).

5. See how a show is produced by joining a live audience or attending a taping of a pilot show.

6. Determine the characteristics of the American family as shown in a popular drama or situation comedy series (size, relationships, distribution of authority, attitudes toward money).

7. Survey students and parents for an estimate of their total time weekly before a TV set.

8. Conduct your own analysis of audience for
   (1) TV as the major source of information on news, sports, weather, or entertainment;
   (2) each channel (Seek the public television audience especially.);
   (3) TV specials (news, documentaries, theater and music, social and political issues, children's shows, variety entertainment).

9. Soap-opera stereotypes    What feelings and attitudes do you experience when you separate the good guys from the bad guys?
   Do the emotions of a character change when he identifies a bad guy?
   What are the separate conflicts of the major characters? To what extent do those separate conflicts overlap? Who that you know in real life has any of these same conflicts?
   Simulate the next day's episode, acting carefully in character. (Are there actions or emotions that are difficult for you to act?)

64

*Dramatic Reality*

1. What electronic and medical equipment does the public learn to accept as parts of regular programs dealing with adventure, crime, and medicine?

2. What freedom from law do the main characters exercise that is open to indictment in real life?

3. What legal protections that exist in reality for the accused are bypassed on TV?

4. What official positions in society are identified as being held by major characters in dramas? (If they are not identified, what dramatic purpose is served by their not being in conventional employment?)

5. What effects does music have on time and space?

6. What effects do camera techniques and film speed changes (stop-action, slow-motion) have on time and space?

7. Write a job description for your favorite television dramatic character (doctor, lawyer, super-sleuth).

*The Game Plan*

1. Do the rules of the game depend on competition, skill, knowledge, or chance? (Analyze the requirements for becoming a contestant on a variety of game shows.)

2. Why is the game played at all(contestants, sponsors, audience, budget, etc.)?

3. What kinds of information about themselves and/or others are contestants willing to reveal for what kinds of rewards?

4. Who sponsors what kinds of shows, when, and why? (What are the sponsoring products? Who is in the viewing audience? How much presentation time does each product get? Are prizes equal for games of the same name in the afternoon and in the evening?)

5. Does the live audience laugh at or with the contestants?

6. What insights would contestants get from seeing a rerun of their own performance?

7. What are the general qualifications in attitude, voice, appearance, personality, and acting ability that game-show MC's seem to share?

8. What values in American society would a foreign visitor identify if he judged only by a game show or game shows in general?

66

9. What game shows would you like to participate in? (Why?) reluctantly participate in?
(Why?)

10. Are there game shows you would refuse to
participate in? (Why?)

11. What game shows do you watch regularly?
(Why?) occasionally? (Why?) never? (Why,
if for a reason other than scheduling?)

12. Is your watching of game shows primarily of
those you would or would not participate in?

*Mass-Media Literacy*

Today a person who learns from only one
medium will to some major degree lack the
information, interpretation, insight, and expression that permit society to deem him
literate. A literate person needs the greatest
possible contact with the largest possible
number of points of view and sources of
information. And beyond that, he needs to
develop the power, in turn, to express himself.

If a man depends solely on print for his
information and his contact with creative
literature, he cannot keep up with the hap-
penings of the world without submitting, at
least partially, to the biases that inevitably
filter fact on its way to print. And he limits
his interpretation of literature to his own
capacity for imagination.

If a man depends solely on radio for his news, his music, and his drama, he slows his intake to the speed of sound; he accepts information schedules exterior to himself and he restricts, simply by time, the variety of points of view he can sample. He also suspends his own potential capacity for interpreting literature in favor of hearing the interpretations of others.

If a man depends solely on film for his access to information and ideas, films are always out of date for current events and they are an expensive means of access to interpretation by others.

If a man depends solely on television, he limits his knowledge of current events predominantly to what took place within camera range, to the visible and spoken action of world and local leadership, and to the selection by cameramen and cameras and editors and officials and sponsors whose limitations he cannot know but whose biases he is subjected to without their identification. And he must content himself with being a passive observer of most television fare unless he phones in to a talk show.

The mass-medium-literate man must see for himself as much as he can on television and test what people say there against what he sees. He must listen to radio at least enough to remain aware of the diversity of taste and attitude that typify segments of his local community. He must read a daily newspaper or two, at least with some thoroughness so that he can rethink what he has seen and heard and, again, test the validity of others' opinions. Furthermore, he must find those news items too small or too specialized themselves to demand time on the air or in the eye. Then he must read magazines and books to put both immediate news in detailed perspective and the present in relation to the past. In his spare time he should improve his mind with books and film and TV drama and live concerts.

He is not a literate man, however, until he acts beyond the act of thinking. If he can create in print or film or video or paint or music or some other medium, he should. If he cannot create, he should criticize. If indeed the real work of man is growing to be literate, he has a responsibility to use his knowledge at least in part to shape in turn the media that shape him.

## ACROSS MEDIA

### Reading Context

1. Where is print? (Collect as many different locations as possible — trucks, cans, boxes, buildings.)

2. Compare the order of information in the caption of and in an action news photograph.

(Make a string poster connecting image with word.)

3. Experiment to see if recall is greater on product identification through flashing company names or logos.

4. Analyze political cartoons to see what knowledge from what media are required to understand each one.

5. Prepare ads to introduce a new company or product on radio and TV and in newspapers and brochures to be mailed to the general public.

6. Compare how many ways time and space can be altered in different media.

7. What is the vocabulary of media literacy (film, advertising, TV, computer, papers, magazines, etc.)?

*Medium Literate*

1. How many media can you translate any one thing into?

2. Invite an ad agency representative to explain the media program they have devised for a particular client.

3. Make a chart comparing time and space costs in advertising among local TV, radio, and daily and weekly newspapers; suburban, city, regional, and national newspapers; network

and cable television; local and network radio; local and national magazines.

4. News (Record, in the appropriate medium, TV, radio, and newspaper coverage of one news story for one day. Compare the coverage of the different media.) (Compare the coverage of one continuing issue in mass media for one week.) (Separate fact from opinion in news on radio, TV, newspaper, and weekly news magazines. Compare and contrast the problems involved in the separation.)

5. To be fully informed on current news each week, what media need you use, how often, and why?

6. Survey students to see what proportion have access to what media at home (books, magazines, newspapers, TV, phonographs, tape recorders [reel, cassette, eight-track], cameras [still, movie, TV]). What media do students use for self expression?

7. Find out how cable television can provide two-way communication and for what.

8. Visit local companies to see what computers are doing (telephone, electricity supplier, IBM, Honeywell).

9. What media can computers link? (Visit the computer system in your police headquarters, school system.)

10. Identify what equipment designed originally for space flight is used now every day on earth. (Project what will be adapted next.)

11. How are communications satellites used? By whom? For what?

12. Project the effects of media on life in the year 2000 A. D.

13. What if
    — there were no radio in your community? (What services break down?)

    — there were no telephones in your community? (So what?)

    — there were no print at all in your community? (          )

## Chapter 5: Fail-Safe

About the only permissible reasons for a student not to pass a media course are his own failures to work or to come to class. So long as he is learning to think and demonstrating that he is learning in some acceptable way, he should be passing. The question, of course, is: What is acceptable? And in terms of the evaluation of thought and the growth involved, *acceptable* doesn't translate easily into *A*s, *B*s, and *C*s.

Since media teaching is primarily the assisting of a student in thinking about his own ideas in his own direction, the individualization of work makes grading almost impossible in any traditional form. Therefore, more than in any other course perhaps, the student must participate in determining his grades.

Only the student knows the degree of his benefit from the course. And almost always that benefit is not of the sort he would

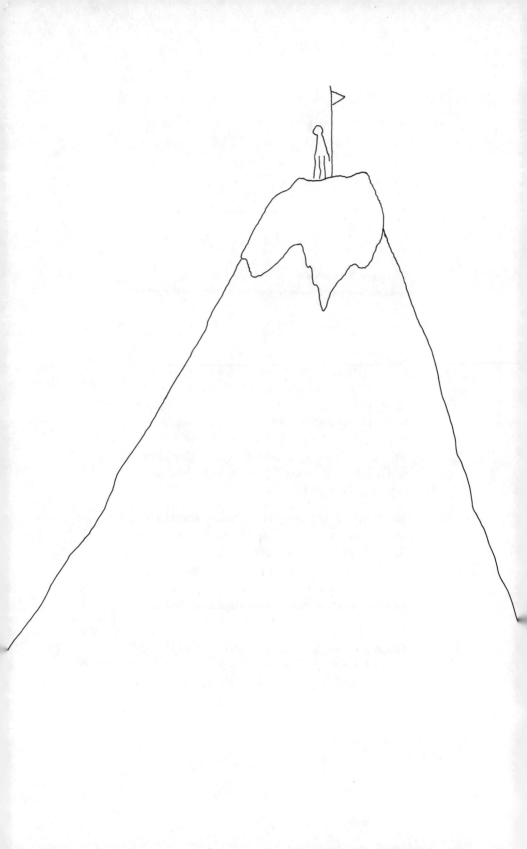

conventionally expect from a traditional class. He will seldom have learned an objective body of fact the mastery of which by itself deserves credit. He seldom will perform enough consistent experiments in learning that the quantity of work alone deserves credit. Surely he will see that time spent is not enough to qualify for credit either.

Hopefully, the student will know what personal skills and what academic tools he has learned to apply to the integration of his own life experience. Media class may be the first integrative group and integrative work of his school career. Particularly in those circumstances, only he can know how well he has gotten together himself, his academic knowledge, and his understanding.

Most grades that students give themselves can be accepted by the teacher. If there is an important discrepancy between what the teacher and the student believe is fair, the reasons for the differences should be talked about in private individual conference. Such discussion especially helps those students who have never recognized their own creativity or who have been consistently considered mediocre in traditional performance. Given the opportunity to judge his work in relation to its value to him personally, such a student often cannot give himself a good grade without outside help in changing his view of himself as a failure.

If students are to grade themselves, each will need to develop standards of judgment relative to his individual and group abilities and information. What quantity of work has been done? How hard has he worked and how long? How has he worked in comparison with the person who didn't come often to class and in comparison to his best friend? What is the quality of his work? Has he grown as a thinking human being?

If it has to be translated into a grade, satisfactory learning alone may be worth an *A* for the student whose competence and experience are extremely limited to begin with. On the other end of the scale, there should be no *A* for an exceptionally qualified student unless he exhibits originality and inventiveness in addition to performing whatever minimum level of activity is established by the class in combination with the teacher.

Media is a perfect course for a contract system. Ideally, the teacher and the individual student agree on the kind, quantity, and quality of work he will do for a particular grade. Because the student agrees to a performance he chooses, the responsibility for learning shifts to him, and the teacher becomes properly the student's consultant. Furthermore, from the grading itself the student learns. Sometimes he learns not to underestimate his ability when he does excellent work but contracts for a *B* and gets it.

Sometimes he learns to accept responsibility for going ahead and finishing an unrealistic quantity or quality of work. Always he learns something about the relationship between his real learning and what is externally observable.

Performance contracting can remove the fear of failure from the student who has severe learning problems and remove the guarantee of effortless success from the student who has exceptional endowments of talent and/or background. Any student who attempts to do something which for him is difficult, or new, and which extends his experience will earn a C even if his work falls short of his intention and his contract. Some plan for successful communication with his classmates should be a part of the contract of any student who seeks an A. In return for that effort, he can expect commentary, help, and evaluation of his work by the class.

Perhaps what makes the media curriculum potentially most failure proof is the opportunity the class affords for independent individual work within group projects. The media teacher can deliberately mix students to add experience to those who lack it, give support to those who need it, and make demands on those with special skill. What often emerges are exciting revelations of individual capacities frequently masked in standard performance.

 For example, in heterogeneous classes there usually are at least one or two students who are emotionally disturbed enough to be a problem to themselves and others. In a project where group success requires work with others, such students often perform remarkably well. If their responsibility is either independent but essential to the group's success or if they have authority to direct others in an activity where they themselves have some facility, other students will accept the deviant students and their contributions. And that acceptance often helps stabilize those students' whole school day.

If students are given choices to match themselves with one another, the chances are that disruptive students nevertheless will choose and be chosen to work very productively in a group project. In fact, to be accepted enough to be permitted to cooperate in the accomplishment of something that they care about, they often will find out things about themselves that may have favorable influences on their behavior from then on. Furthermore, the variety and the individualization of media projects — even the specific assignments of persons within groups — permit so much satisfaction to each individual that often a student can accommodate even to persons who ordinarily exclude him or whom he usually rejects because they threaten him.

In many ways media teaching is extremely hard. Every student sooner or later challenges the teacher to help discover interests to explore and to devise activities with which to explore them. Because of the freedom that must be allowed students, those interests also often lie outside the teacher's personal range or experience. Furthermore, even when students do their own grading, evaluation of student work requires constant finding and accepting of new ways to look at both learning itself and media products. Even an experienced teacher will have to experiment constantly to permit and handle the flexibility of assignments, organization, and behavior that student freedom to grow literate requires.

## Chapter 6: Caterpillars and Tadpoles

Metamorphosis is nature's way of translating a tadpole into a frog or a caterpillar into a moth. Yet, tadpoles are not frogs, and no one mistakes caterpillars for butterflies. Sometimes metamorphic changes occur in increments small enough to be individually invisible even though they all occur under observation. Sometimes the major changes occur so completely beyond observation that one must be told that what went in and what came out are the same in basic nature though different in form.

When an entomologist identifies the caterpillar of a monarch butterfly, he knows with certainty both that it is not some odd sort of worm and that it will proceed through very predictable steps. Watching it gorge itself on leaves, this insect specialist knows that in time the caterpillar will shape its cocoon, grow through its pupal stage, and emerge full grown in the perfect yellow, orange, black and white patterns of its kind.

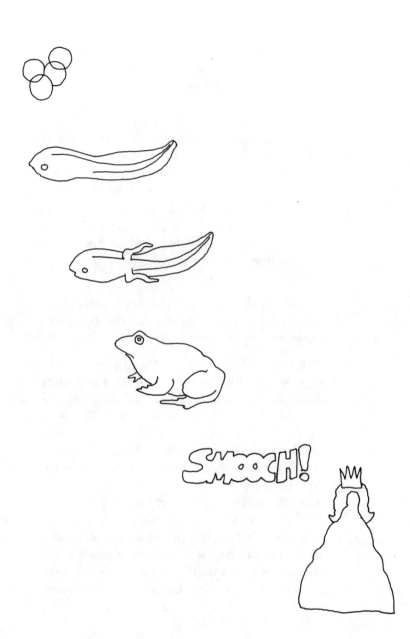

The process of translation exercised by a human being is not so predictable or so automatic as metamorphosis. The genetic code of the frog or butterfly decrees each step of its cycle. No such automatic biological system operates the mind of man when it transforms something from one medium to another. For example, translation of a short story is thought of as traditionally taking place in the same medium – language, as from French to German – rather than as a change of form. But a short story has nothing in its nature that will prevent its being translated into film or its inspiring music.

Despite their essential difference, translation and metamorphosis have a number of useful parallels.

The changes that come upon a tadpole occur very slowly and result in visible continuous reshaping toward a form to some degree already basic to the legless tad. The new product of human translation often also involves visible adaptations of the original. A translator of a short story from one language to another will keep the general organization and the major content of the words of the original. He will change only the sentence structure that makes the sense fall naturally into the patterns of the second language. He will make as few modifications of the sense as he can within the limits of the second vocabulary. In fact, the original and the translation still will be called "a" short story despite the transformations involved in turning one into the other. Nevertheless, they may be as different as tadpole and frog. More significantly, the precise process by which the skillful translator modifies or amends the original to produce the same or greater perfection in the new medium are as hidden in the human mind as the program for the emergence of the frog's hind legs is hidden nature.

Translation from the medium of language to the medium of music or of sculpture is much more like the metamorphosis of a butterfly than like that of a frog. The changes that come upon a caterpillar are visible in stages, but the pupal part of the process is completely hidden. Both metamorphosis and translation from one medium to another involve keeping involate the innate identity of the original while changing the outward form entirely.

Human physical growth fits the analogy neither of the frog nor of the butterfly. However, the growth of a human mind has analogies to both. Mental growth proceeds invisibly at its own rate in its natural way much as the butterfly develops beyond observation. But evidences of mental growth are as observable as the gradual appearance of frog's legs. For example, we know gurgles and coos will become intelligible speech.

We accept the natural developments of insects and frogs. No one will poke a tadpole, say "hop," and stand back to see an instant frog obey. Nor will any sane man order his bagworms to emerge as monarch butterflies. The frog will naturally grow from the tadpole if he has even a mediocre quality of frog environment, though the adult frog may wear a vestigial tail for a long time.

Many an adult human being keeps the appendages of childhood long after they are expected to disappear. If we have no patience with them, we sometimes amputate both external behavior and physical appendages we do not approve in human beings. However, natural mental development occurs beyond our sight. If an adult mind is to emerge, it will follow its nature, and its nature only. What internal effects do our external amputations have?

Consider the possibility that translation is the process by which a person becomes himself. Sometimes he takes others' attitudes, feeds on them, hides his digestion of them out of sight in his mind, and emerges invisibly but permanently different from what he was before he listened. Another time he translates his energy into grades or athletics or thoughtfulness or bullying the block — whatever gets him the best results from the persons he admires most. Each time he takes an idea, an action, a purpose and translates it into thought, action, or creation, he changes himself.

How does a human being develop spending habits? Is he simply made so fat with propaganda or commercials or beliefs that he goes into a mental cocoon and, after an incubation period, comes out a buyer? If, unlike a butterfly, he learns the processes that operate on him, can he choose what kind of buyer he will become?

## ROUND AND ROUND

### Translate into words

1. a short story into a ballad

2. a poem into a paraphrase

3. a formal menu into standard English

4. your life into a three-page autobiography

5. an idea into a poster or collage

6. road signs into language

7. erosion into figurative processes (as "facial erosion")

### Translate into film

1. (animate) a wheelie, print cartoons, a process

2. ethnic culture into photographs

3. a song into a drama

4. a drama into a silent film

5. night traffic into time-exposures

6. the history of a place (photographs of a main street)

*Translate into art, graphics*

1. an emotion to images

2. words into colors

3. wire, metal scraps into sculpture

4. make a poem concrete

5. a bar of soap into sculpture

6. a picture into a silk screen poster

*Translate into numbers*

1. a physics principle into a mathematical formula

2. a filled grocery cart into dollars and cents

3. linear into metric measurement

4. inches into picas

5. pieces of wood into a cabinet

6. input into computer language

*Translate into maps*

1. a school floor plan into a texture map for blind students

2. population density into a map (texture, color, pattern, contour)

3. location of industries

4. traffic flow — through town, to and from work

*Translate into music*

1. time into a march

2. a poem into music

3. color, emotion into music

4. any work from major to minor, vice versa

5. tempo within a song into another

*Translate into time*

1. a trip to Mars, Jupiter, etc.

2. sun's shadows

3. high school

4. dreams during sleep

5. yourself aged 10, aged 30, aged 70

6. becoming a welder, contractor, a pharmacist, a lawyer

7. starlight

*Translate time into*

1. a flow chart of any process

2. money for a secretary, a bricklayer, a lawyer, a bank teller

3. travel by foot, car, train, plane, rocket

4. milk (ask a goat for help)

*Collect the translations of others*

1. migration of continents (Australia, New Zealand)

2. maps on any subject

3. computer art, poetry

4. paintings (Ask local artists to exhibit original work)

5. crafts (Find local talent to teach skills using wood, metal, sewing, leather, herbs)

6. geometric patterns of the movement of fusion, planets, plants, extra-terrestrial radio signals, Jupiter's magnetic field

7. logos and symbols (from newspaper ads, classified, signs on buildings, TV) (Objects with symbolic meaning [apple; flags] )

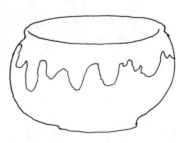

*Inside out*

1. Do a cut-a-way of an engine, a body, any structure.

2. Cut in two a geode, a saphire, a cell.

*Symbol Making*

1. Make logos for rooms in the school.

2. Make signs to direct the deaf around your school.

3. Draw safety signs for shop areas in schools.

4. Diagram how to work any machine by labeling and numbering each part in order of its use.

5. Make symbols for occupations, sports, etc.

6. Substitute seriality for tonality in a familiar musical work.

7. Make flow charts of cycles (life, water, air, chain reactions, life cycles of stars).

8. Study, in physics, new designs for storage. (Study rings in electron-proton accelerators.)

*Compare Look-Alikes*

1. grafts in plants and transplants in humans

2. volcanos and guisers

3. geologic and biologic metamorphosis

4. cycles and chain reactions

*Commentary*

1. Write conversations or comments that might be said by persons, animals, or objects in pictures cut from magazines and newspapers (by public figures about current events)
   —(by babies with adult ideas)
   —(by animals with human postures, facial expressions)
   —(by trees, lakes, flowers about the environment)

2. Reconstruct American society in 1975 from five objects found on an archaeological expedition in 4000 A.D.

3. Cover an historical event of the past (signing Magna Carta) with current media used in reporting today's news.

4. As a minstrel of 1000 A.D., compose a ballad about the facts of a current news event.

5. Graph world population using figures from ten years intervals to the present, and project them twenty years into the future.

6. Decide if adaptation is a form of translation (example: Alaska's Snow Monkeys)

## Chapter 7:
## I'm Uninformed, You're Ignorant, He's Stupid

In a time of impending material shortage, a government spokesman announces with pride the foresight of officials in building up the government's inventories. At the same time he chides big business for stockpiling the same material. And if the housewife is in on the act, he accuses her of hoarding. The housewife meanwhile knows that she is shopping wisely but agrees that business should be called down for creating an artificial shortage and attacks the government for manipulating the economy. The businessman calls a news conference to point out that maintaining materials in sufficient supply keeps the gross national product growing but urges that the government get out of competition with the private sector. He calls on the housewife not to do panic buying, since the shortage anticipated will be at most a temporary effect of the law of supply and demand.

Each person is speaking about the same material, the same shortage, and the same method of guarding against going without. Yet each sees his own practice as justified even while he finds fault with others. Each, that is, sees primarily his own point of view.

The tendency to speak as commendably as possible of one's self, slightly less well of someone who is at least present to defend himself, and negatively of persons well beyond earshot is a human habit if not human nature. The safeguard against blind assurance that all the rest of the world is out of step is to keep aware of how many different points of view there can be in a given situtation.

Point of view is a term having to do on a literal level with the physical position from which one can see. What one sees from a balcony differs considerably from what the

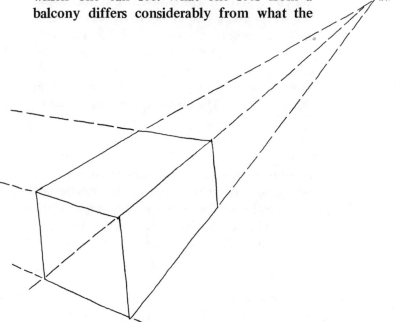

same person sees from a hang glider or a sky-lab. The same kinds of differences in perspective are illustrated by looking at an ant with the naked eye, a magnifying glass, and first an optical and then an electron-scanning microscope. The greater the perspective, the less the detail. The greater the detail, the less the perspective. e. e. cummings suggested that in that sense "electrons deify a razor blade into a mountain range."

*NB*

Point of view is much more than physical, either in relation to place in space or to ability to see. Point of view is affected at least as much by time and experience and psychology and biology and involvement. A junior high school student is probably going to be rather sure an adult is nuts if the adult tries to sell him that these are really the happiest days of his life. But that same student may listen to a great-grandfather's stories about life on the farm during the Great Depression and think how wonderful it would be to have lived in those good old days.

In literature, point of view is much simpler than in real life. In fact, literary point of view can be determined rather precisely once the narrator of a story is identified.

There are three narrators who tell their stories in the third person — about others without themselves having any relation to the action. If the narrator stays out of the story but knows all past and present history and can

come and go in space and time and can read
the minds and emotions of all the characters,
he is an omniscient (all-knowing) narrator. If
he really is omniscient but for some literary
purpose chooses to limit what he tells to what
a major character in the story has the sight,
insight, and ability to know, the narrator is
called a limited-omniscient narrator. If he tells
only what an intelligent fly could see and hear
and knows nothing outside his two senses or
the time and place when and where he
observed, he is an observer narrator.

There are also four narrators who tell their
stories in the first person — about themselves
to some degree. A narrator who tells stories
others have told him (hearsay reporting, tall
tales, etc.) is a first-person narrator-at-second-
hand. If he tells a story in the first person
about himself as it occurs, he is a present
participating narrator and therefore has no
more (and perhaps less) insight into what is
happening to him than the reader has. If he
tells the story of his life as he looks back over
it, usually with considerably greater insight
than he had when the events he tells about
were happening, he is a first-person retrospec-
tive narrator. If he tells the story of someone
in whose action he was a minor character, he
is considered a first-person observer narrator,
but he may have either advantages or disad-
vantages that stem from his involvement in
the action.

It is hard enough to determine in a fixed form
like literature just what the abilities, limitations, and attitudes of a narrator are. In real
life, we often are so involved in thinking of
ourselves as the center of all the actions
important to the universe that we identify
neither our own points of view nor those of
others. To learn to know ourselves, to learn to
know others, and to learn to be literate about
media, we should devise means for changing
our points of view. Physics suggests that an
infinite imaginary line drawn from any point
will curve until it returns to its starting point.
Therefore, any tiniest motion in space will
change the entire course of that curving line.
If we can learn to move left and right, in and
out from the earth — if we can look through
all manner of windows with every contour of
glass — if we can hear the inaudible with the
help of magnification — if we can remove our
senses and study the effect on our total
perception — then we can at least begin to
understand ourselves better because we understand our time and space and energy relationships better.

Our human relationships require different
changes that are no less — perhaps are even
more — important. Can we change our minds?
Quite literally, can we imagine having less or
more mind than we have? Can we substitute
for what we have absorbed from our culture
or our physical environment both the rich-
nesses and the poverties we would have

enjoyed/suffered had we been born elsewhere or elsewhen? Can we dream the dreams of others, fear their fears, hate their hates — even if who and what we are already are the objects of those others' dreams and fears and hates? If not, what's the point of having any view?

## FROM WHERE YOU STAND

### Lose Your Senses

1. You have just had — a frontal lobotomy, a heart attack.

2. You have just lost your sense — of touch, taste, sight, smell, kinesthesia.

3. Lose your most creative talent and perform without it.
   (If you are an artist, become color blind.)
   (If you are a writer, lose your grammar.)
   (If you are a musician, become tone deaf.)
   (If you're logical, give up order.)
   (If you're not physically disabled, become so — turn in one foot and walk without a limp.)

4. Add the one character trait you wish you had the most. (Practice your new image before a mirror and pantomime it for the class.)

*Choose: Them or Us?*

1. Without a kidney transplant you will die.

2. If you get the transplant, a 35-year-old woman with two children will die.

3. Divide this year's production of wheat, books, radios, TV's, cars by this year's world population.

4. You have three children and find out that another baby is coming.

5. You want to finish school, and you're pregnant.

6. You want to finish school, and the girl you've been dating is pregnant.

7. Your son is looking for a job and you own a business.

8. You see a purse in an empty room.

9. You want a promotion and find a mistake your supervisor has made.

10. You have a chance to go out with your best friend's steady.

11. The smartest student in class sits in front of you at the exam.

12. Everybody else has tried it once.

13. As soon as you pull into the right lane after passing on an interstate, the car you passed pulls out to pass you.

14. A person of another race invites you to a concert.

*So?*

1. Using a newspaper story, tell what happened from the points of view of everyone involved. (Assign parts and practice separately.)

2. Would you sign a contract containing these?
   to some degree
   more or less
   to a certain extent
   within reason
   with deliberate speed
   beyond a reasonable doubt

3. Photograph the same place from ground level, a tree or similar height, and from a building overlooking the site.

4. In any literature, establish the point of view of the narrator. Change to a different narrator.

5. What's new on Venus, Jupiter, Mars, the moon, etc.?

6. Move to a new school where you don't know as much as the others.

7. View the 1973 eclipse in Africa as a scientist and as a tribal native.

8. Who lives at the top and bottom of the hill(s) in your town?

9. Look at a city ghetto from a street in it and from the top floor of the nearest condominium.

10. Fill out the form for receiving food stamps as the official, then as the applicant.

11. Why do you want to be tall?

12. What is the significance of the difference between the ratios of single men and women now and ten years ago?

13. What are biological sex differences?

14. What are sociological sex expectations?

15. How old is young? Old? Mature? Legal?

*Action-Reaction-Retraction*

1. She's taller than he is.

2. You're too young . . . .

3. No son of mine . . . .

4. But she's not like the rest of them.

5. They all look alike.

6. She's smart enough to be quiet.

7. That's one thing you can count on.

8. I tried so hard . . . .

9. He didn't tell me.

10. I should . . . but . . . .

11. Be rational.

12. I don't know what to do with . . . .

13. That's an emotional response.

14. How much experience have you had?

15. What I mean is . . . .

16. Now back where I come from . . . .

17. What I can do for you is . . . .

18. It's just a . . . .

19. These irresponsible . . . .

20. It's just not a ____ I like.

21. Handsome devil.

22. That's not practical.

23. I did what I was told.

24. Don't ask stupid questions.

25. That wasn't my job.

26. They like to live like that.

27. She's going to keep the baby?

28. . . . too lazy

29. What kind of____?

30. Of course you'll graduate.

31. They'll outgrow that.

32. He's really not her type.

33. He's hooked.

34. The little woman

35. My old man

36. My old lady

37. The better half

38. The breadwinner

39. It's only a job.

40. It's just money.

41. I got it for nothing.

42. The view alone is worth it.

43. Every man has his price.

44. It doesn't mean a thing.

45. I don't care . . . .

46. . . . right out of the jungle

47. If you don't love it, leave it.

48. Look what's happened to the neighborhood.

49. a woman's place

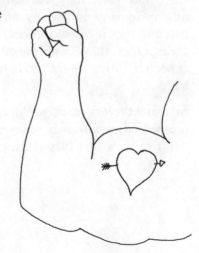

## Chapter 8: The Tiger and the Lady

There was a young lady of Niger
Who smiled as she rode on a tiger.
They returned from the ride
with the lady inside
And the smile on the face of the tiger.

— Unknown

A great many things in life and literature and history and science depend on what might be termed situation reversal. What goes up must come down. A muscle flexed must relax. Energy can be detected as light or sound or mass and each may be converted into the other. Comedy is tragedy at a distance and without moral consequences. Irony is either saying one thing and meaning another or expecting one thing and having another happen.

In almost every case, what appears to be a reversal of situation is really a limitation of point of view or a focus on a part instead of a

whole — attention paid to one phase of a cycle or one state of matter.

One out of five romances in popular women's magazines for years has depended on unexpected collisions. A beautiful young girl leaves her apartment with her arms loaded with garbage intended for the trash shute around the corner. A handsome young man heads from that corridor for the elevator on her hall. At the corner, they collide and romance springs to life as he helps her collect her old banana peels. All that would be needed to save the situation would be one maintenance engineer standing on a ladder changing a light bulb at the intersection of the halls. He could call a warning, the young people would avoid their collision, she would go on safely with her garbage and he would catch his elevator without event. The whole short story business could be wrecked with a few well placed observers.

Another way to do-in television, radio, stage, and screen is simply to have everyone change his schedule. If the boss never comes to dinner, it won't matter that the oven won't cook. If the thief breaks into the right apartment a year late, the masterpiece will be safely hung in the museum.

Changes of place serve the same function. If the detective shows up on the wrong series, the murderer can't be caught. And what would happen to war if the enemies ended up ready to fight but in different countries?

Changes of mind can reverse almost any situation. Deciding not to go fishing may save the life of an innocent dolphin. Turning off the television may interrupt the best laid plans of Madison Avenue.

No matter how sophisticated we become, we will constantly be dealing with situation reversal — in our minds, in our perceptions, in our creations, and in our communications. As observers we can alter our relationships in space and time sufficiently to get the perspective that lets us learn from others without permanent pain and often with pleasure. As participants, we are far more likely to stumble into situations that reverse themselves or that we reverse. Sometimes we fall into reversals because we see too much on too grand a scale. At others, we see too much in too great detail. Often our stumbling leads to our physical harm but more frequently to the injury of our pride. If we can develop a sense of humor, we can learn to share the view of ourselves that others have. That ability to see ourselves as others do will help us laugh and so have the emotional distance to handle the damage or the recognition that we gain from reversals that affect our egos.

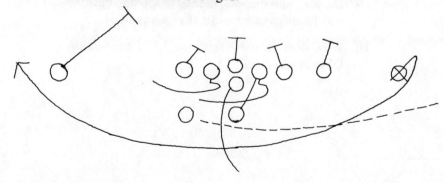

*INSIDE OUT*

*What If?*

1. Collect comic strips where the last frame is a situation reversal of expectations in motion, time or action.

2. Collect comic strips where the words contribute to the situation reversal.

3. Change the timing when characters meet during the opening minutes in any short story or drama on TV or in print.

4. Change the setting where characters meet in any . . . .

5. Stop-action during any TV program or literature to predict the reversal that will produce the final resolution.

6. Write one line gags for comedians.

7. See what children learn from cartoons that reverse real-life. (setting, motion, time, space, size, physics, animal and human behaviors)

8. Collect comics that comment on society and politics (Doonsbury, Butter and Boop, Conchy, Peanuts, Pogo, L'il Abner, Little Orphan Annie, political and editorial cartoons).

9. In the newspaper, identify sports, business and front page reversals that made news.

10. Why does a baby first laugh? (Photograph. Observe. Record.)

*What Are the Odds?*

1. Study your playing of a game or sport. (How many reversals do you make? How many does your opponent make? Who wins?)

2. Analyze the statistics of a football game — punts, interceptions, fumbles, etc.

3. What are the mathematical probabilities that gambling will "pay off"?

4. How do open secrets feel about the invasion of their privacy?

5. Find reversals in
   collecting experimental evidence
   astronomical explorations
   computer projections
   any war
   physics
   evolution
   genetics
   propulsion
   agression in animal and human behavior
   magic
   TV programs

6. Make comic strips by reversing the last frame.
   (Reverse movement.)
   (Use a size or time switch.)
   (Add a play on words or verbal irony.)

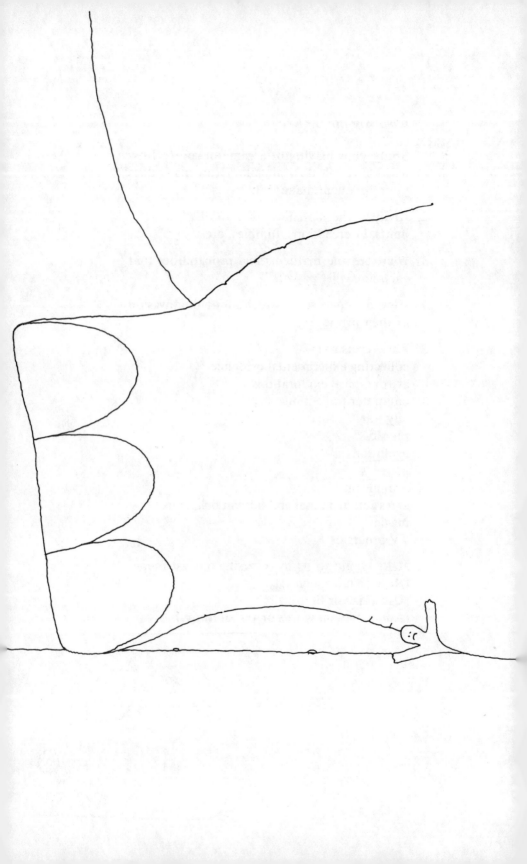

## Chapter 9: What's the Best Way to Get Out from Under an Elephant?

The question "What's the best way to get out from under an elephant?" can finally be answered by one of two people: an observer or someone who's under one. Meanwhile, don't worry about how he got there or why. Just willingly suspend your disbelief. There really is somebody under an elephant.

Get it clearly in your mind that a human being is being sat upon. There is not someone merely beneath that elephant. That person has a real 2,000-pound problem. Now decide: Is that somebody you or someone else? Which you are makes all the difference.

If you have let someone else be under the elephant, you know yours was not a generous decision. Given a him-or-me choice like that, almost anyone would let someone else go first.

So there he is under the elephant. What's the best way to get out? You have chosen to observe, perhaps even to assist. But it's not really your problem. At least technically, that makes you objective. Since you are not involved in such energy-consuming activities as breathing under pressure, you can concentrate either on recording the behavior of the sat-upon or on devising ways and means for extricating him. Your detachment permits you also to weigh the relative merits of processes and devices for removing either the elephant or the person. There is nothing in the question "What is the best way ..." to make you responsible for the person himself. To the uninvolved, the "best" inevitably means method or manner, not condition. You cease to be objective in your interpretation of the question the second you become involved — begin to care. Objectivity calls for the suspension of judgment of values unless "values" translates as "most efficient," "most effective," "most economical," etc.

*NB*

The greater your involvement, the less your objectivity and the less your concern with how to get out from under the elephant. In fact, if you are the person under the elephant, you are enormously involved. From a position under an elephant, "the best way to get out from under" is alive. And that answer is a judgment concerned totally with condition. Any method that will work will do. Your intellectual interest in the quality of method decreases in direct proportion to your concern with survival itself.

A great deal has been said about the desirability of objectivity and the undesirability of subjectivity. Reality — as opposed to the purely theoretical — suggests that total objectivity is a quality potential to computers and that subjectivity is an inevitable part of every human judgment.

Suppose you are given an elephant and power over even your worst enemy. Inviting the elephant to be seated on him is, at its most objective, accompanied by delight at the picture. Pleasure is scarcely objective. However, something in the nature of human consciousness will not permit you to let even the imaginary elephant remain seated very long. No matter how unworthy a person you deem your enemy (two value judgments: unworthy and enemy), you inevitably judge also his worthiness to remain alive. In a moment of fantasy — you are as free as is ever possible to deal with a person objectively and dispassionately. Yet as human being you will inevitably set limits on the degree of damage you are willing to do.

Scientists have tried as hard to be objective as any single group of persons concerned with ways and means. Yet repeatedly their great discoveries have come because they were involved with other, and/or their environment. That involvement was so great that, when the apple fell or when the mold grew or when the red cells were devoured by the white, they cared. That subjective involvement has constantly pushed back the limits within which objective exploration is possible. It drives the experimenter to repeat and repeat and repeat his experiement — not to prove its perfection, but to find its flaw — the crack through which he sees what no one ever saw before.

Next time you have a choice about who will decide the world's important questions of value, snatch the opportunity to be the one who thinks his way out from under an elephant. The more your survival and that of others is the question, the less will be your concern for analysis and the more for life itself. The less survival is a question, the more room there will be for the logical analysis that is the hallmark of objectivity. But room for objectivity does not mean that subjectivity is less desirable. The subjective provides the drive that creates the opportunity for the objective.

*"THERE IS A TIME FOR EVERY THING UNDER THE SUN."*

1. ice
2. volcanos
3. peneplaining
4. mountain-building
5. birth
6. death
7. peace

8. war
9. love
10. hate
11. youth
12. age
13. stages of matter

*Hide-and-Go-Seek*

1. magnification and reduction
2. appearance and reality
3. matter and anti-matter
4. hallucination
5. amnesia
6. ESP
7. UFO's
8. projection (missles, film, and people)
9. sublimation (gases and people)

*Where Is It? What's in It? Who's in It? Why?*
*(Note: "When" for all the question should be*
*the same.)*

1. photos of the school

2. maps (road, density, topography, etc.)

3. buildings (jails, churches, hospitals, businesses)

4. collections (stamps, coins, etc.)

Now switch the "when."

*Who Is Who?*

1. Who owns what in property and ideas? (me, mine; his, hers; our, ours; yours; theirs – in stories, political speeches, etc.)

2. Who owns the most? (Count possessive pronouns)

3. Who is important? Who is the narrator? (Is it told by an "I" or about "them"?) Who is the major actor? (Who is the subject of the most verbs?) Who uses the biggest words? the most complex sentence structure? the greatest number of assertions of opinion as if they were fact? So what?

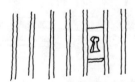

*Hair Line*

1. fracture (skull x-ray)

2. faults

3. bomb sights

4. wigs and hair pieces

*Draw the Line*

1. court lines (tennis, volleyball)

2. field lines (magnetic, land)

3. time (date lines, time zones, deadlines)

4. vectors

5. right and wrong (role play)

6. black and white

7. spectrum

8. referee any game

*Sending and Receiving*

1. computer banks (libraries, cable TV)

2. telecommunications

3. satellites, cables, and space labs

4. transporters (horses, cars, trains, rockets, lasers, minds)

5. time (transmission speeds, secret and delayed messages)

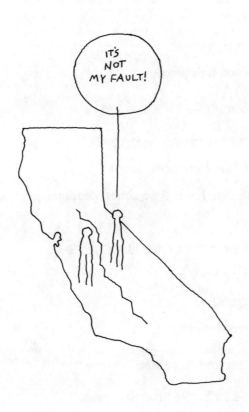